Contents

un coca

une eau minérale

un coca light

une limonade

un jus d'orange

un Orangina

Les boissons

un thé

un café

1

Écrire les boissons en français: (Write the drinks in French:)

1)

✏️ *un thé*

2)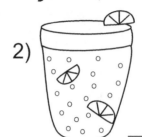

_____

3)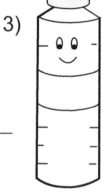

_____

4)

_____

_____

5)

6)

_____

7)

_____

un jus d'orange - an orange juice   un coca light - a diet coke

une limonade - a lemonade   une eau minérale - a mineral water

un thé - a tea   un café - a coffee   un coca - a coke

Au café (At the cafe)

Je voudrais _____, s'il vous plaît.
(I would like a _____, please.)

Lire les phrases et dessiner les boissons:
(Read the sentences and draw the drinks:)

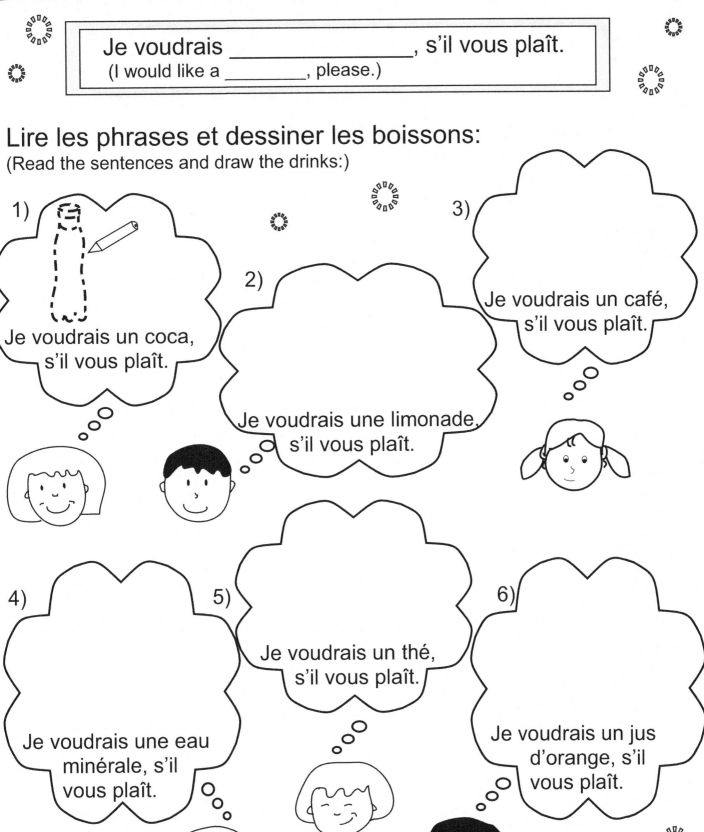

1) Je voudrais un coca, s'il vous plaît.

2) Je voudrais une limonade, s'il vous plaît.

3) Je voudrais un café, s'il vous plaît.

4) Je voudrais une eau minérale, s'il vous plaît.

5) Je voudrais un thé, s'il vous plaît.

6) Je voudrais un jus d'orange, s'il vous plaît.

3

Qu'est-ce que vous voulez? (What do you want?)

> Je voudrais _____, s'il vous plaît
> (I would like a _____, please)

Commander ces boissons. Écrire les phrases en français:
(Order these drinks. Write the sentences in French:)

1) *Je   voudrais   un   coca,   s'il   vous   plaît.*

_____ _____ _____ _____, ____ _____ _____.

2) _____ _____ _____ _____, ____ _____ _____.

3) _____ _____ _____ _____, ____ _____ _____.

4) _____ _____ _____ _____, ____ _____ _____.

5) _____ _____ _____ _____, ____ _____ _____.

6) _____ _____ _____ _____, ____ _____ _____.

7) _____ _____ _____ _____, ____ _____ _____.

| un coca | un café | un thé | une limonade |
| un orangina | un coca light | une eau minérale | |

Combien y en a-t-il? (How many are there?)

Compter les boissons. Combien y en a-t-il?
(Count the drinks. How many are there?)

six _____ limonade**s**

_____ coca**s**

_____ jus d'orange

_____ thé**s**

_____ café**s**

_____ eau**x**

1	2	3	4	5	6	7	8	9	10
un	deux	trois	quatre	cinq	six	sept	huit	neuf	dix

5

Les boissons (drinks)

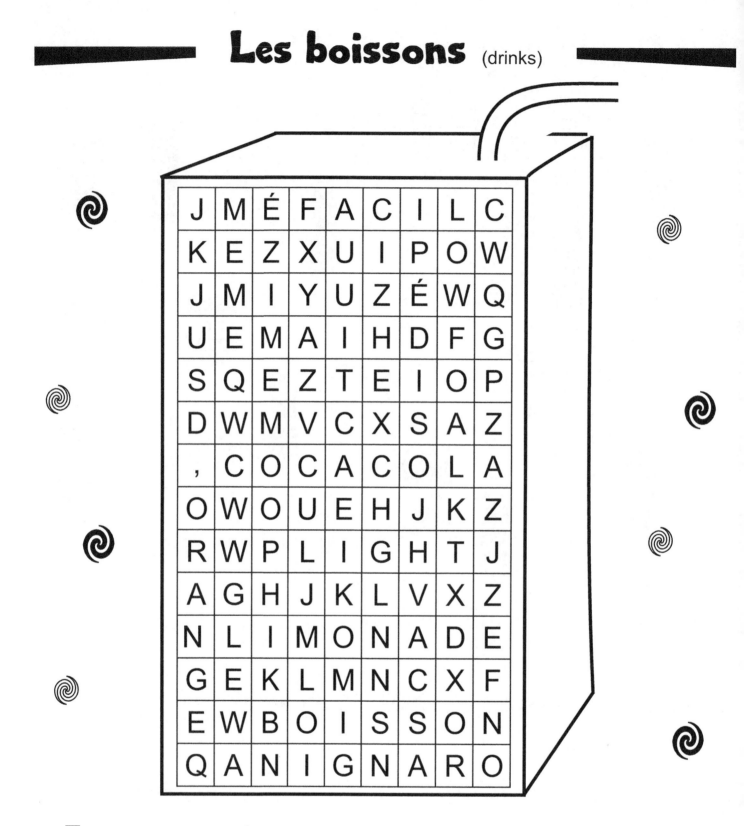

J	M	É	F	A	C	I	L	C
K	E	Z	X	U	I	P	O	W
J	M	I	Y	U	Z	É	W	Q
U	E	M	A	I	H	D	F	G
S	Q	E	Z	T	E	I	O	P
D	W	M	V	C	X	S	A	Z
,	C	O	C	A	C	O	L	A
O	W	O	U	E	H	J	K	Z
R	W	P	L	I	G	H	T	J
A	G	H	J	K	L	V	X	Z
N	L	I	M	O	N	A	D	E
G	E	K	L	M	N	C	X	F
E	W	B	O	I	S	S	O	N
Q	A	N	I	G	N	A	R	O

Trouver ces mots: (Find these words:)

LIMONADE	THÉ	CAFÉ
COCA-COLA	EAU	LIGHT
ORANGINA	BOISSON	JUS D'ORANGE

une pomme

une orange

une banane

une fraise

une poire

Les fruits

un kiwi

un citron

un melon

Les fruits (fruit)

Copier les mots et les dessins: (Copy the words and the pictures:)

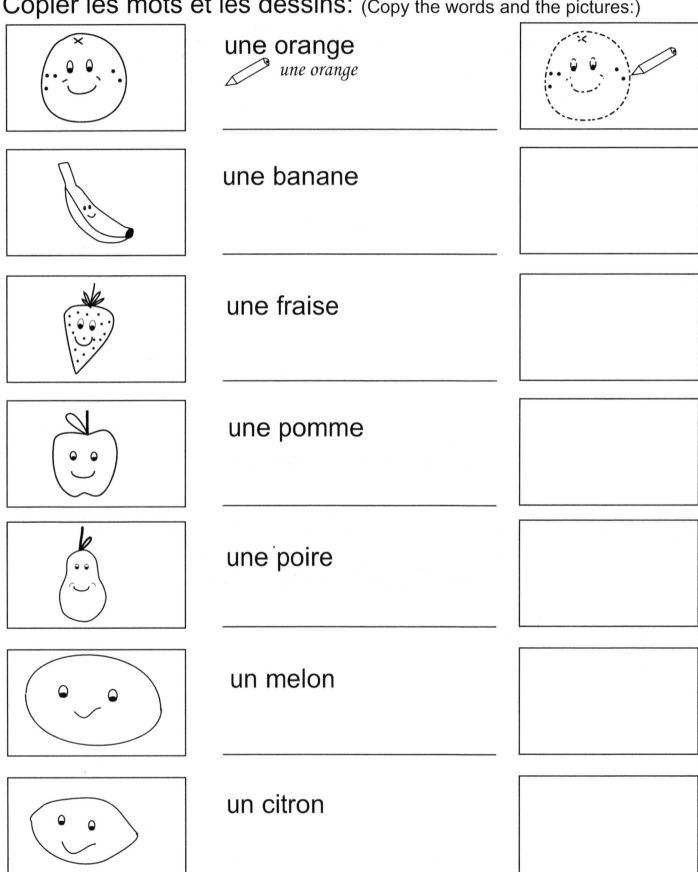

une orange
✏ *une orange*

une banane

une fraise

une pomme

une poire

un melon

un citron

8

C'est masculin ou féminin?
(Is it masculine or feminine?)

In French some words are masculine (boy words) and some words are feminine (girl words). This does **NOT** mean that some words are only for boys or girls. It just means that it is important to recognise and remember if to say "a" you use **un** or **une** before the words:

Écrire les fruits dans la boîte correcte. (Write the fruit in the correct box.)

Masculine words (un)

Feminine words (une)

une banane

une orange

un citron

une fraise

un melon

une pomme

une poire

un kiwi

9

C'est de quelle couleur? (What colour is it?)

Colorier les dessins: (Colour the pictures:)

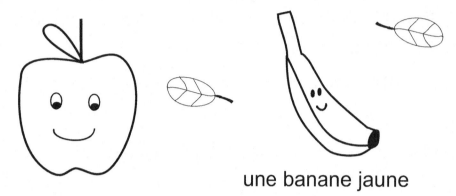

une pomme rouge

une banane jaune

In French the colours go AFTER the noun:

vert ……….green

rouge ……..red

jaune ……. yellow

marron ….. brown

un kiwi marron

une fraise rouge

un melon vert

un citron jaune

une pomme verte

Notice how **vert** has an extra **e** on the end for the fruit which start with une.
(Femimine words)

une poire verte

10

Combien y en a-t-il? (How many are there?)

Dessiner la quantité exacte: (Draw the correct quantity:)

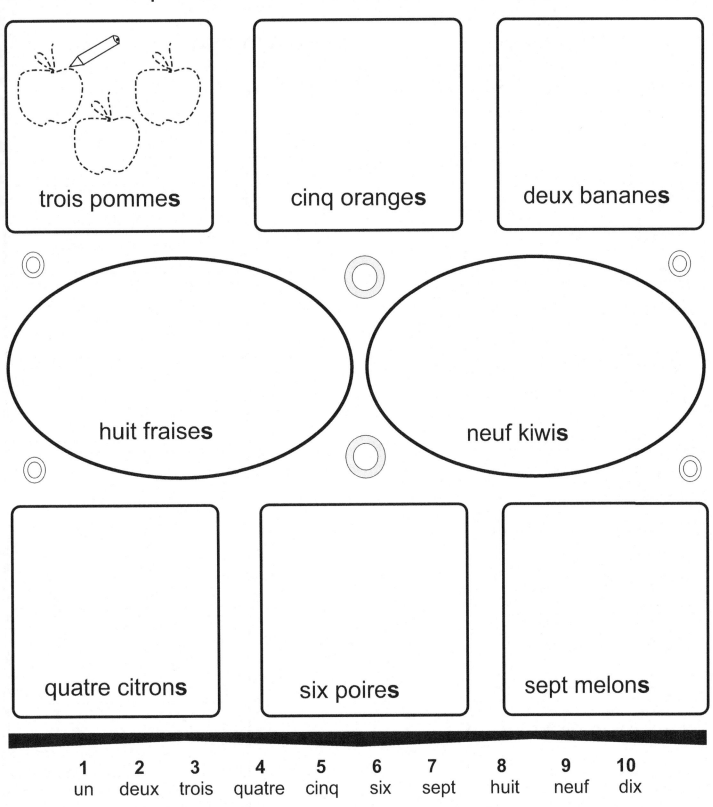

trois pomme**s**

cinq orange**s**

deux banane**s**

huit fraise**s**

neuf kiwi**s**

quatre citron**s**

six poire**s**

sept melon**s**

1	2	3	4	5	6	7	8	9	10
un	deux	trois	quatre	cinq	six	sept	huit	neuf	dix

fraises - strawberries   citrons - lemons   poires - pears   pommes - apples

oranges - oranges   bananes - bananas   kiwis - kiwis   melons - melons

11

Tu aimes les fruits? (Do you like fruit?)

J'aime (I like)

Je n'aime pas (I don't like)

Relier les phrases et les dessins: (Match the phrases to the pictures:)

Je n'aime pas les pommes.	
J'aime les poires.	
J'aime les oranges.	
J'aime les fraises.	
Je n'aime pas les poires.	
Je n'aime pas les bananes.	
J'aime les bananes.	
J'aime les pommes.	
Je n'aime pas les oranges.	

12

Qui aime les fruits? (Who likes fruit?)

Salut!
Je m'appelle Sophie.
J'aime les pommes et les poires.
Je n'aime pas les fraises.
Salut!

   Sophie

Salut ……….......Hi / bye

Je m'appelle…….My name is

J'aime ………......I like

Je n'aime pas ..….I don't like….

Salut!
Je m'appelle Marc.
J'aime les bananes et les oranges.
Je n'aime pas les poires.
Salut!

   Marc

Salut!
Je m'appelle Anne.
J'aime les fraises et les kiwis.
Je n'aime pas les bananes.
Salut! **Anne**

Lire les lettres et compléter le tableau:
(Read the letters and complete the table:)

	🙂 Fruit they like	🙁 Fruit they don't like
Sophie		
Marc		
Anne		

Les fruits

```
U P O M M E Z
M K E I T V E R T I
J H R R I R O U G E R I
I Y I M U K S E S I A R F
L O M R K R E E C B M X Z
P W F M K G X N I X A I E G
L K G H N V O N T M R W D E
T U M A J L X D R W R I A
I T R V E X D E O W O K X
O M M K U Y T N X N S
T Y E N A N A B F O
U J A U N E P
```

Trouver ces mots: (Find these words:)

une **POIRE**

une **POMME**

une **FRAISE**

une **BANANE**

une **ORANGE**

un **FRUIT**
(a fruit)

un **MELON**

un **CITRON**

MARRON
(brown)

VERT
(green)

ROUGE
(red)

In French there are two different ways of saying our word "a" : un, une.
These words do not appear in the word search.

14

douze

treize

quatorze

quinze

onze

Les numéros 11 - 20

seize

vingt

dix-sept

dix-neuf

dix-huit

Combien y en a-t-il? (How many are there?)

a)

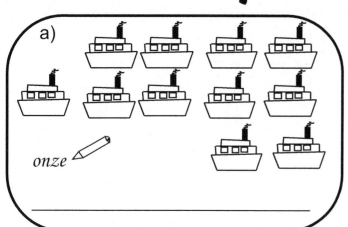

onze ✏️

_____

b)

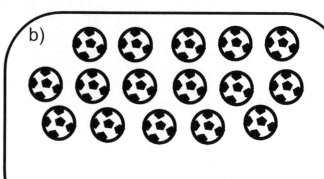

_____

c)

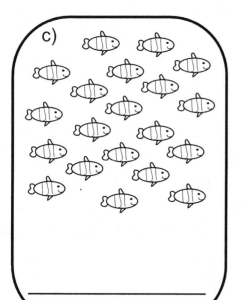

_____

d)

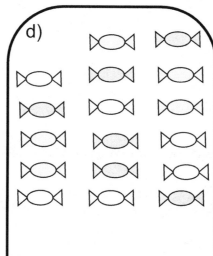

_____

e)

_____

f)

_____

g)

_____

11	**12**	**13**	**14**	**15**	**16**	**17**	**18**	**19**	**20**
onze	douze	treize	quatorze	quinze	seize	dix-sept	dix-huit	dix-neuf	vingt

C'est quel numéro? (What number is it?)

1) Relier les numéros aux mots: (Match the numbers to the words:)

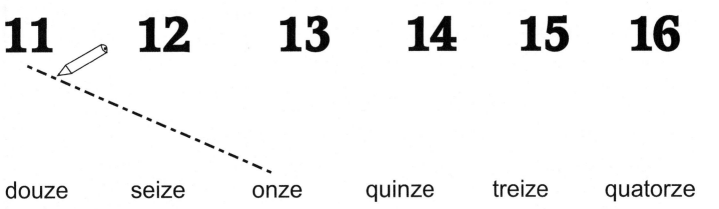

11   **12**   **13**   **14**   **15**   **16**

douze   seize   onze   quinze   treize   quatorze

2) Écrire les numéros en français: (Write the numbers in French:)

a) **18**   *dix-huit*

_____

b) **20**

_____

c) **17**

_____

d) **16**

_____

e) **19**

_____

11	12	13	14	15	16	17	18	19	20
onze	douze	treize	quatorze	quinze	seize	dix-sept	dix-huit	dix-neuf	vingt

C'est de quelle couleur? (What colour is it?)

Colorier le numéro vingt en bleu clair.

(Colour the number 20 in light blue.)

Colorier le numéro douze en vert foncé.

Colorier le numéro seize en marron clair.

Colorier le numéro dix-huit en bleu foncé.

Colorier le numéro onze en marron foncé.

Colorier le numéro treize en gris clair.

To say if a colour is light or dark, after the colour you have **clair** for light and **foncé** for dark:

bleu clair — light blue
gris clair — light grey
vert foncé — dark green
bleu foncé — dark blue
marron clair — light brown
marron foncé - dark brown

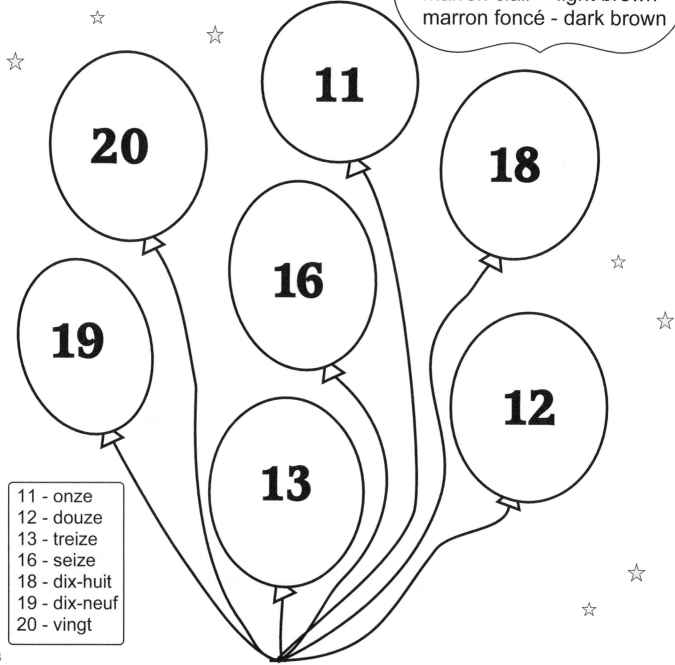

11 - onze
12 - douze
13 - treize
16 - seize
18 - dix-huit
19 - dix-neuf
20 - vingt

Les numéros 1 - 20 (numbers 1-20)

Remplir les numéros qui manquent: (Fill in the missing numbers:)

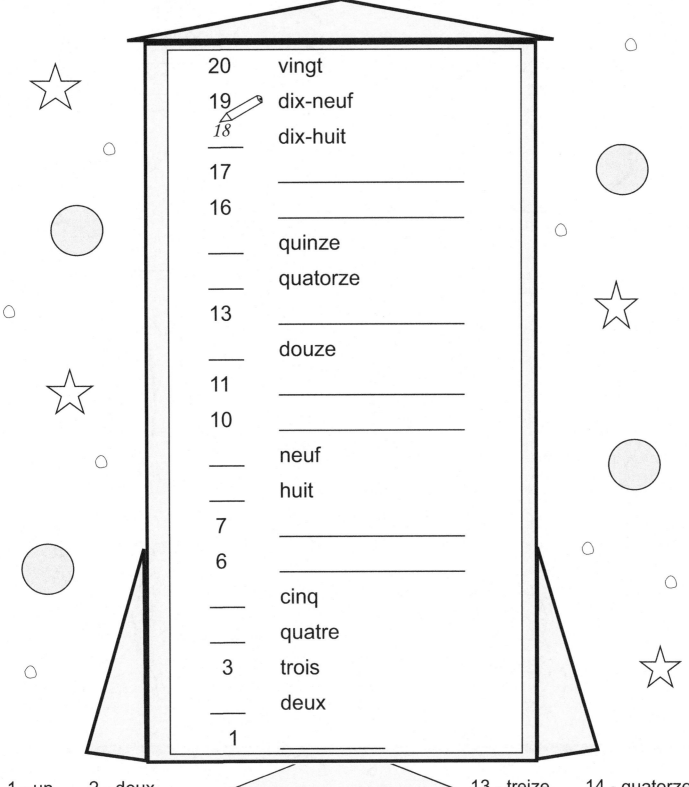

20	vingt
19	dix-neuf
18	dix-huit
17	_____
16	_____
___	quinze
___	quatorze
13	_____
___	douze
11	_____
10	_____
___	neuf
___	huit
7	_____
6	_____
___	cinq
___	quatre
3	trois
___	deux
1	_____

1 - un   2 - deux
3 - trois   4 - quatre
5 - cinq   6 - six   7 - sept
8 - huit   9 - neuf   10 - dix   11 onze   12 douze

13 - treize   14 - quatorze
15 - quinze   16 - seize
17 - dix-sept   18 - dix-huit
19 - dix-neuf   20 - vingt

19

Les maths (maths)

Faire les calculs: (Do the calculations:)

dix-neuf
- douze
_____
sept

_____

treize
+ trois
_____

_____

onze
+ six
_____

_____

seize
+ trois
_____

vingt
- dix-huit
_____

quinze
+ cinq
_____

vingt
- neuf
_____

dix-sept
- cinq
_____

quatorze
- un
_____

	1	**2**	**3**	**4**	**5**	**6**	**7**	**8**	**9**	**10**
	un	deux	trois	quatre	cinq	six	sept	huit	neuf	dix
	11	**12**	**13**	**14**	**15**	**16**	**17**	**18**	**19**	**20**
	onze	douze	treize	quatorze	quinze	seize	dix-sept	dix-huit	dix-neuf	vingt

Les numéros 11 - 20

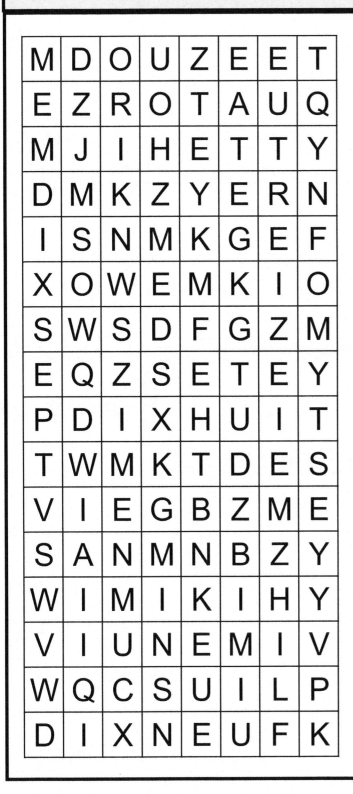

M	D	O	U	Z	E	E	T
E	Z	R	O	T	A	U	Q
M	J	I	H	E	T	T	Y
D	M	K	Z	Y	E	R	N
I	S	N	M	K	G	E	F
X	O	W	E	M	K	I	O
S	W	S	D	F	G	Z	M
E	Q	Z	S	E	T	E	Y
P	D	I	X	H	U	I	T
T	W	M	K	T	D	E	S
V	I	E	G	B	Z	M	E
S	A	N	M	N	B	Z	Y
W	I	M	I	K	I	H	Y
V	I	U	N	E	M	I	V
W	Q	C	S	U	I	L	P
D	I	X	N	E	U	F	K

Trouver ces mots:
(Find these words:)

11 ONZE

12 DOUZE

13 TREIZE

14 QUATORZE

15 QUINZE

16 SEIZE

17 DIX-SEPT

18 DIX-HUIT

19 DIX-NEUF

20 VINGT

il pleut

il y a du soleil

il neige

il fait froid

il fait chaud

Le temps

il fait mauvais

il fait beau

Le temps (the weather)

Copier les phrases et faire un dessin:
(Copy the phrases and draw a picture:)

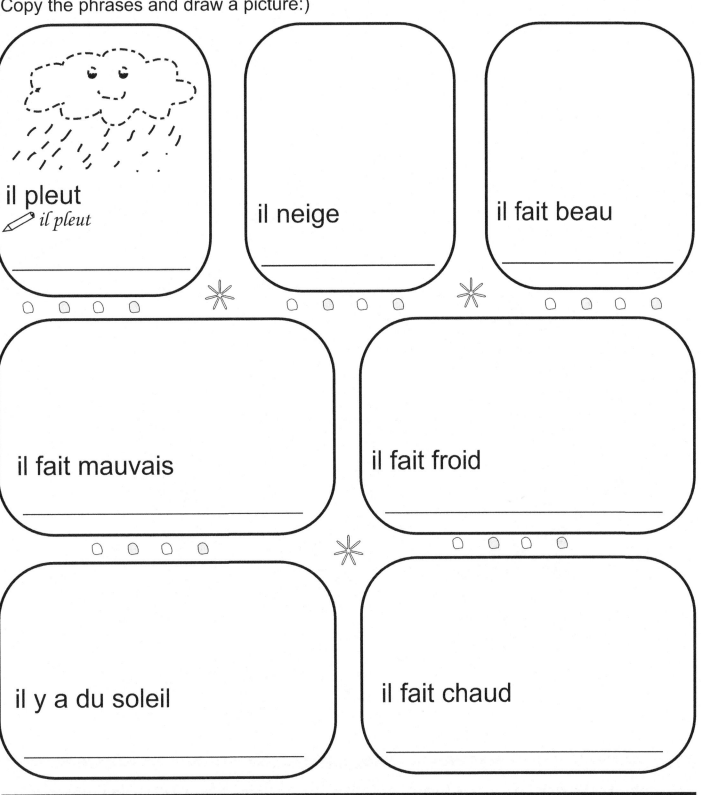

il pleut

il pleut
_____

il neige
_____

il fait beau
_____

il fait mauvais
_____

il fait froid
_____

il y a du soleil
_____

il fait chaud
_____

il pleut - it's raining   il neige - it's snowing   il fait chaud - it's hot   il fait beau - it's good weather

il fait froid - it's cold   il fait mauvais - it's bad weather   il y a du soleil - it's sunny

23

Quel temps fait-il? (What is the weather like?)

Écrire les phrases pour le temps en français:
(Write the phrases for the weather in French:)

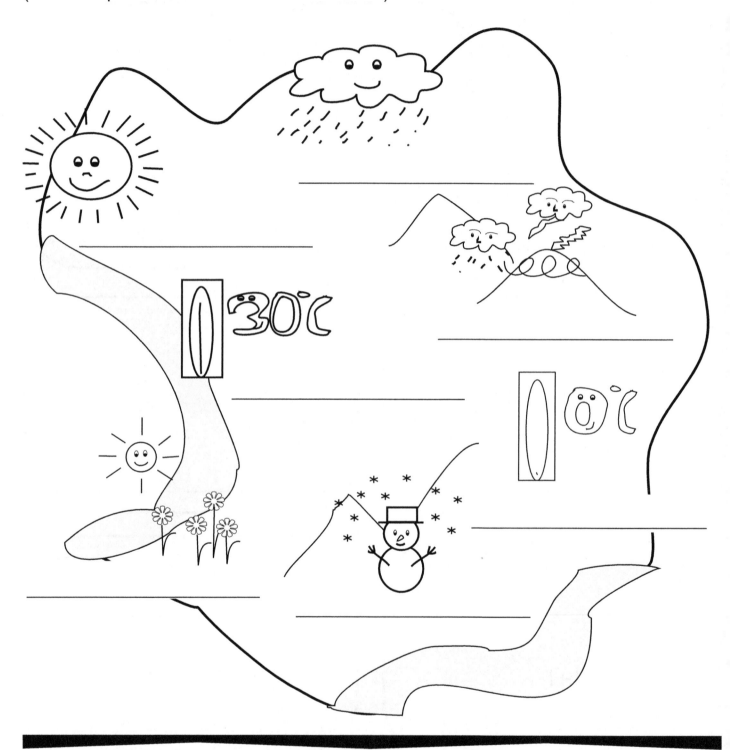

il pleut - it's raining   il fait chaud - it's hot   il fait beau - it's good weather

il neige - it's snowing   il fait froid - it's cold   il fait mauvais - it's bad weather

il y a du soleil - it's sunny

Où habites tu?
(Where do you live?)

| Salut .... Hi / bye |
| J'habite à .... I live in ... |
| J'aime .... I like... |
| Aujourd'hui...... Today |
| mais .... but |
| et .... and |

Salut!	Aujourd'hui il fait froid
J'habite à Paris!	mais il y a du soleil.
J'aime Paris!	Salut! Marc

Salut!	Aujourd'hui il fait froid
J'habite à Lyon!	et il neige!
J'aime Lyon!	Salut! Anne

Salut!	Aujourd'hui il fait chaud
J'habite à Nice!	et il y a du soleil!
J'aime Nice!	Salut! Sophie

Lire les cartes postales et répondre aux questions:
(Read the postcards and answer the questions:)

Sophie

1) Who lives in Nice? _____

2) Who says it is cold but sunny? _____

3) Who says it is hot and sunny? _____

4) Who lives in Lyon? _____

5) Who likes Paris? _____

6) Who says it is snowing? _____

7) Who says it is cold? _____ and _____

25

Les jours de la semaine (The days of the week)

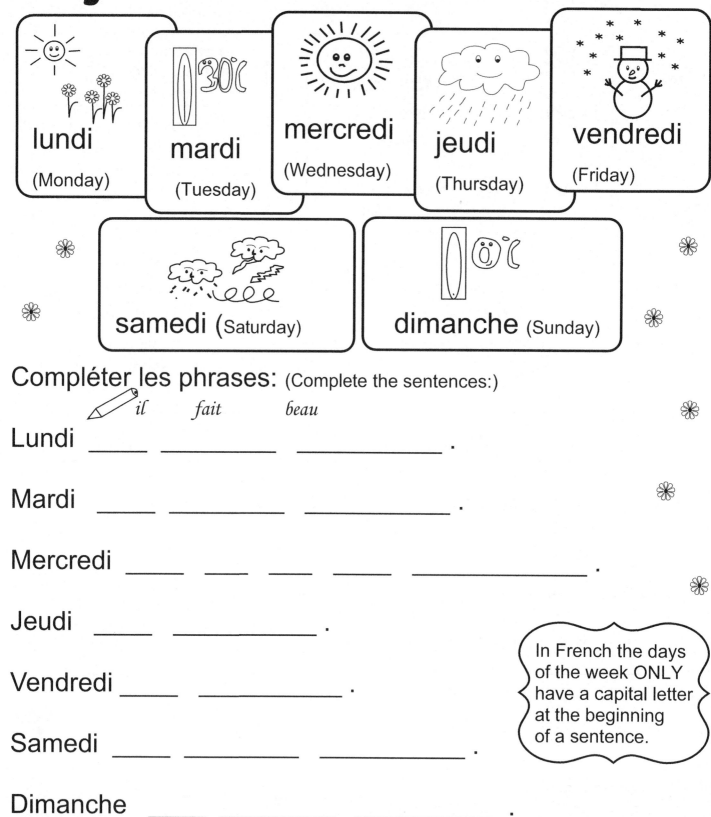

lundi (Monday)

mardi (Tuesday)

mercredi (Wednesday)

jeudi (Thursday)

vendredi (Friday)

samedi (Saturday)

dimanche (Sunday)

Compléter les phrases: (Complete the sentences:)

il   fait   beau

Lundi _____ _____ _____ .

Mardi _____ _____ _____ .

Mercredi _____ ___ ___ ___ _____ .

Jeudi _____ _____ .

Vendredi _____ _____ .

Samedi _____ ___ _____ .

In French the days of the week ONLY have a capital letter at the beginning of a sentence.

Dimanche _____ _____ _____ .

il pleut - it's raining   il neige - it's snowing   il fait chaud - it's hot   il fait beau - it's good weather

il fait froid - it's cold   il fait mauvais - it's bad weather   il y a du soleil - it's sunny

La météo (The weather forecast)

Relier les boîtes: (Match the boxes:)

Lundi il neige.	Friday 
Mercredi il neige.	Sunday 
Vendredi il y a du soleil.	Tuesday
Samedi il y a du soleil.	Monday
Lundi il fait froid.	Monday
Mardi il fait froid.	Saturday
Dimanche il fait chaud.	Thursday
Mardi il pleut.	Wednesday
Jeudi il pleut.	Tuesday

Lundi - Monday   Mardi - Tuesday   Mercredi - Wednesday   Jeudi - Thursday
Vendredi - Friday   Samedi - Saturday   Dimanche - Sunday

Le temps (the weather)

Trouver ces mots: (Find these words:)

30 c
CHAUD

SOLEIL

IL PLEUT

LUNDI
(Monday)

MARDI
(Tuesday)

BEAU

MAUVAIS

0 c
FROID

IL NEIGE

SAMEDI
(Saturday)

```
I L P L E U T
I M K I U O P S X I F
I L Y V A X Z I M D J L C
W N R E T V A X E Z I Q H L
I E B O P V V M G D H K A I
W I V C U D A S N W Z E U R
O G P A M S K U W E Z S D
E M E R T L Z I D R A M
W F R O I D E R T U
S O L E I L
```

un pull

un t-shirt

un manteau

un jean

un short

un pantalon

les vêtements

une robe

une jupe

une casquette

Qu'est-ce que c'est? (What is it?)

Écrire les mots en français: (Write the words in French:)

1)

un short

2)

_____

3)

_____

4)

_____

5)

_____

6)

_____

7)

_____

8)

_____

9)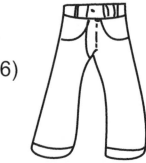

_____

 un pantalon   un short   un jean   un pull   un t-shirt   un manteau   une robe   une jupe   une casquette

C'est de quelle couleur? (What colour is it?)

Colorier en utilisant les couleurs correctes:
(Colour in using the correct colours:)

In French the colours go AFTER the noun.

un t-shirt jaune

un jean bleu

un short vert

un pull marron

un pantalon gris

un t-shirt rose

un t-shirt rouge

un manteau noir

bleu ......blue

gris ....grey

rouge.....red

noir.......black

jaune ....yellow

vert ....green

rose.......pink

marron ...brown

C'est de quelle couleur?
(What colour is it?)

Colorier en utilisant les couleurs correctes:
(Colour in using the correct colours:)

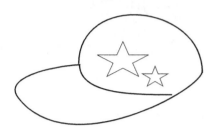

une casquette grise

une casquette jaune

une casquette verte

une casquette bleue

une robe rouge

une robe violette

une jupe noire
et blanche

une jupe rose

Do you remember that some French words are said to be masculine and some words are feminine? Words that start with **une** are feminine and the endings of some colours change when they go after feminine nouns:

bleu / vert / gris / noir : have an **e** added to the end

blanc becomes **blanche**

violet becomes **violette**

Qu'est-ce que tu portes? (What are you wearing?)

| Je porte = I am wearing | Je porte un jean = I am wearing jeans |

Suivre les lignes et écrire les phrases:

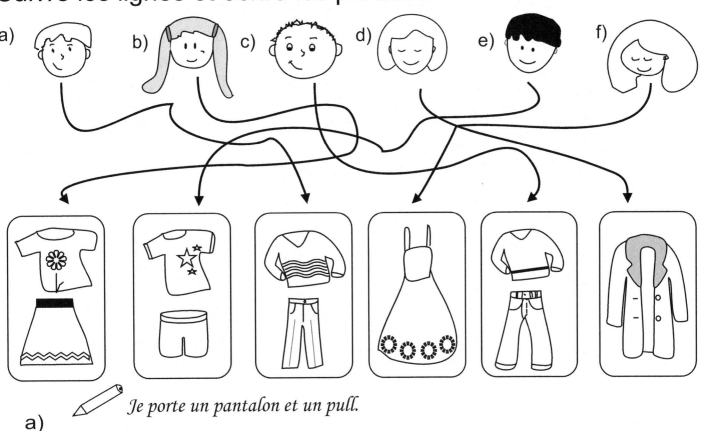

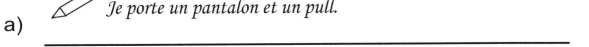
Je porte un pantalon et un pull.

a) _____ .

b) _____ .

c) _____ .

d) _____ .

e) _____ .

f) _____ .

un pantalon   un short   un jean   un pull   un t-shirt   un manteau   une robe   une jupe   une casquette

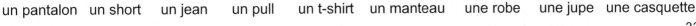

Les vêtements (clothes)

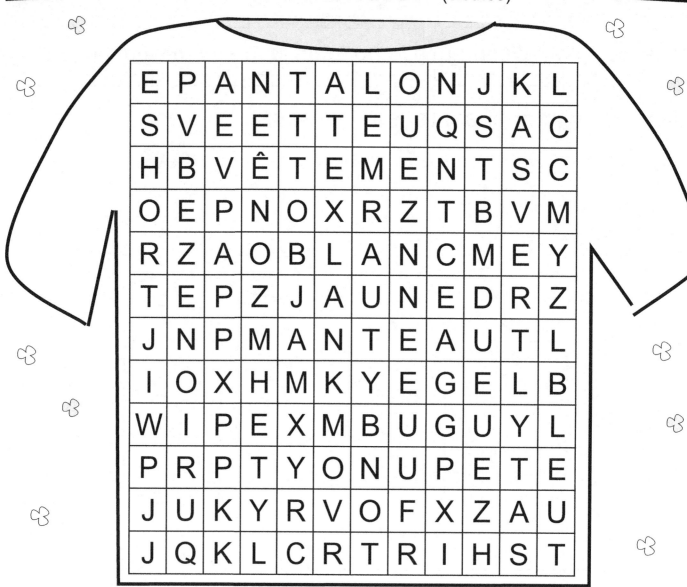

E	P	A	N	T	A	L	O	N	J	K	L
S	V	E	E	T	T	E	U	Q	S	A	C
H	B	V	Ê	T	E	M	E	N	T	S	C
O	E	P	N	O	X	R	Z	T	B	V	M
R	Z	A	O	B	L	A	N	C	M	E	Y
T	E	P	Z	J	A	U	N	E	D	R	Z
J	N	P	M	A	N	T	E	A	U	T	L
I	O	X	H	M	K	Y	E	G	E	L	B
W	I	P	E	X	M	B	U	G	U	Y	L
P	R	P	T	Y	O	N	U	P	E	T	E
J	U	K	Y	R	V	O	F	X	Z	A	U
J	Q	K	L	C	R	T	R	I	H	S	T

Trouver les mots: (Find the words:)

les VÊTEMENTS

BLEU
(blue)

BLANC
(white)

le MANTEAU

le PULL

la JUPE

le JEAN

ROUGE
(red)

JAUNE
(yellow)

le PANTALON

la ROBE

le T-SHIRT

le SHORT

VERT
(green)

NOIR
(black)

In French there are four different ways of saying our word **the** : le, l', la, les.
These words do not appear in the word search.

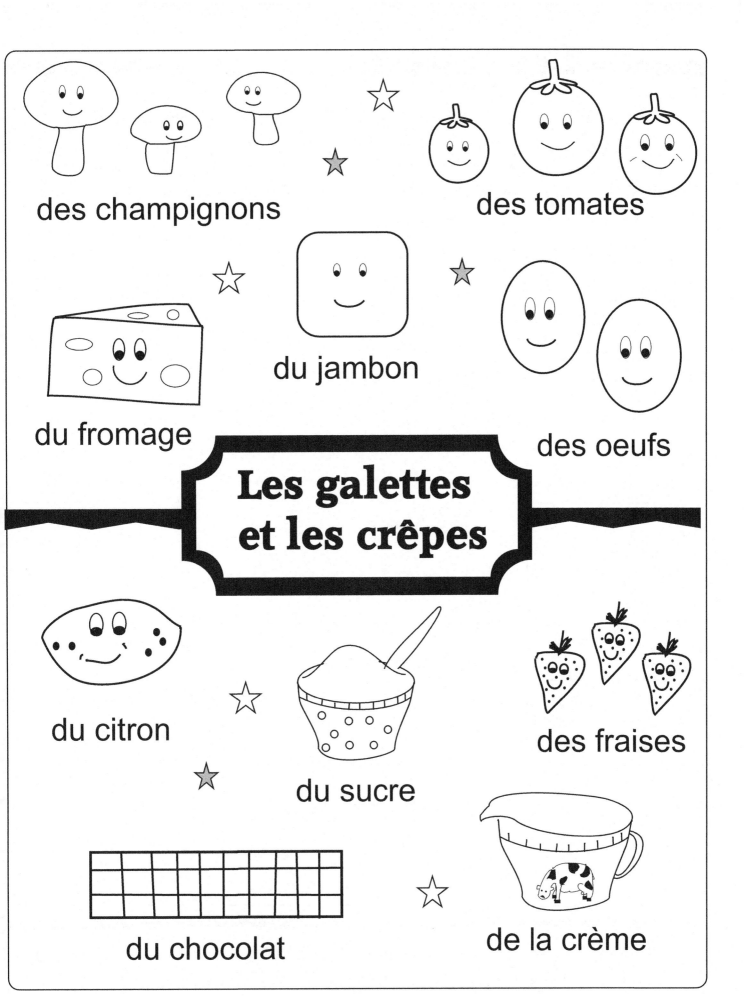

des champignons

des tomates

du jambon

du fromage

des oeufs

Les galettes et les crêpes

du citron

du sucre

des fraises

du chocolat

de la crème

Les galettes (Savoury pancakes)

In France there are lots of places which sell **les galettes.**
Galettes are savoury pancakes made using wholemeal flour.

Copier les mots et les dessins: (Copy the words and the pictures:)

 du fromage

du fromage

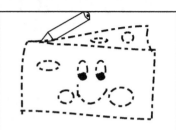

_____

 du jambon

_____

 des oeufs

_____

 des tomates

_____

 des champignons

_____

du fromage - some cheese   du jambon - some ham   des oeufs - some eggs

des tomates - some tomatoes   des champignons - some mushrooms

Je voudrais une galette, s'il vous plaît

(I would like a savoury pancake, please)

Thomas

Je voudrais une galette avec **du fromage** et du **jambon**, s'il vous plaît.

Marie

Je voudrais une galette avec **des tomates** et du **fromage**, s'il vous plaît.

Je voudrais une galette avec **des champignons** et **du jambon**, s'il vous plaît.

Je voudrais une galette avec **des tomates** et **des oeufs**, s'il vous plaît.

Je voudrais une galette avec **du jambon,** du **fromag**e, **des oeufs** et **des champignons**, s'il vous plaît.

Luc

Anne

Paul

Compléter le tableau: (Complete the table:)

	(tomato)	(mushroom)	(cheese)	(ham)	(egg)
Thomas			✓	✓	
Marie					
Luc					
Anne					
Paul					

37

Les crêpes (Sweet pancakes)

In France sweet pancakes are called **les crêpes** and are made using white flour.

1) Écrire les mots en français: (Write the words in French:)

a)
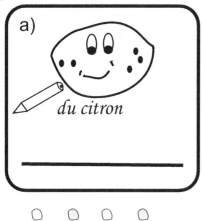
du citron

_____

○ ○ ○ ○

b)

_____

c)

_____

○ ○ ○ ○

d)

_____

e)

_____

2) Réarranger les lettres pour trouver le mot:
(Rearange the letters to find the word:)

a)  *sucre*

R U E C S

du _____

b)

L O A H C T C O

du _____

c)

I R N C O T

du _____

d)

I E S A R S F

des _____

du sucre = some sugar   du citron = some lemon   du chocolat = some chocolate

des fraises = some strawberries   de la crème = some cream

38

Qu'est-ce que vous voulez? (What do you want?)

> Je voudrais une crêpe avec_____ s'il vous plaît
> (I would like a pancake with _____ please)

a)   b)   c)   d)   e)

Suivre les lignes et écrire les phrases:
(Follow the lines and write the setences:)

Je voudrais une crêpe avec du chocolat, s'il vous plaît.

a) _____ .

b) _____ .

c) _____ .

d) _____ .

e) _____ .

du sucre - some sugar   du citron - some lemon   du chocolat - some chocolate

des fraises - some strawberries   de la crème - some cream

Les galettes et les crêpes

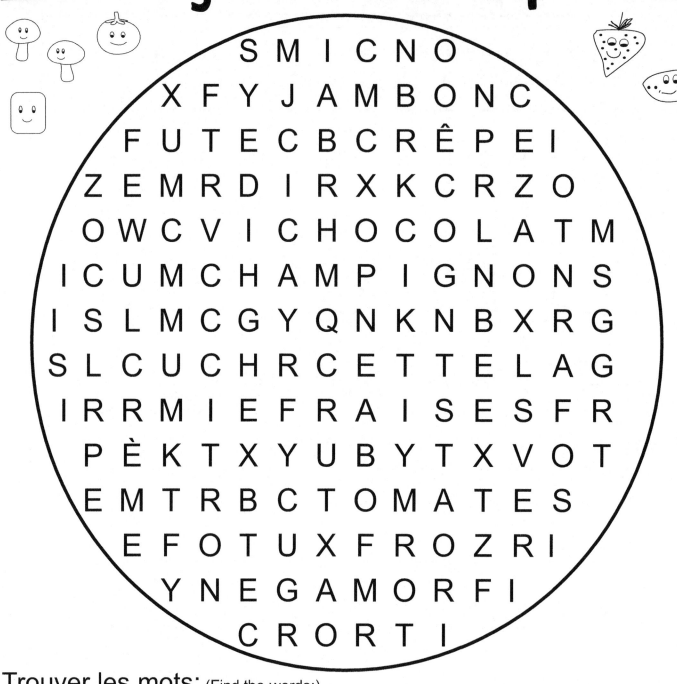

```
        S M I C N O
      X F Y J A M B O N C
    F U T E C B C R Ê P E I
    Z E M R D I R X K C R Z O
    O W C V I C H O C O L A T M
  I C U M C H A M P I G N O N S
  I S L M C G Y Q N K N B X R G
  S L C U C H R C E T T E L A G
  I R R M I E F R A I S E S F R
    P È K T X Y U B Y T X V O T
    E M T R B C T O M A T E S
    E F O T U X F R O Z R I
      Y N E G A M O R F I
        C R O R T I
```

Trouver les mots: (Find the words:)

GALETTE

FROMAGE

JAMBON

TOMATES

OEUFS

CHAMPIGNONS

CHOCOLAT

CRÊPE

SUCRE

CITRON

FRAISES

CRÈME

French		English		French		English	
				j'habite à …		I live in …	
une	banane	a	banana	les	jours	the	days
	blanc		white	une	jupe	a	skirt
	bleu		blue	un	jus d'orange	an	orange juice
les	boissons	the	drinks	un	kiwi	a	kiwi
un	café	a	coffee	une	limonade	a	lemonade
une	casquette	a	cap		lundi		Monday
des	champignons	some	mushrooms	un	manteau	a	coat
du	chocolat	some	chocolate		mardi		Tuesday
	cinq		five		marron		brown
un	citron	a	lemon	un	melon	a	melon
du	citron	some	lemon		mercredi		Wednesday
	clair		light		neuf		nine
un	coca	a	coke		noir		black
un	coca light	a	diet coke	les	numéros	the	numbers
de la	crème	some	cream	des	oeufs	some	eggs
une	crêpe	a	sweet pancake		onze		eleven
un	dessin	a	picture	une	orange	an	orange
	deux		two		orange		orange
	dimanche		Sunday	un	Orangina	a	fizzy orange
	dix		ten	un	pantalon		trousers
	dix-huit		eighteen	une	poire	a	pear
	dix-neuf		nineteen	une	pomme	an	apple
	dix-sept		seventeen	un	pull	a	jumper
	douze		twelve		quatorze		fourteen
une	eau minérale	a	mineral water		quatre		four
	en français		in French		quinze		fifteen
	et		and	une	robe	a	dress
	foncé		dark		rose		pink
une	fraise	a	strawberry		rouge		red
des	fraises	some	strawberries		Salut		Hi / bye
du	fromage	some	cheese		samedi		Saturday
une	galette	a	savoury pancake		seize		sixteen
	gris		grey	la	semaine	the	week
	huit		eight		sept		seven
	il fait beau		it's good weather	un	short		shorts
	il fait chaud		it's hot		s'il vous plaît		please
	il fait froid		it's cold		six		six
	il fait mauvais		it's bad weather	du	sucre	some	sugar
	il neige		it's snowing	le	temps	the	weather
	il pleut		it's raining	un	thé	a	tea
	il y a du soleil		it's sunny	des	tomates	some	tomatoes
	j'adore		I love		treize		thirteen
	j'aime		I like		trois		three
du	jambon	some	ham	un	t-shirt	a	t-shirt
	jaune		yellow		un		one
	je m'appelle		my name is		vendredi		Friday
	je n'aime pas		I don't like		vert		green
	je porte		I am wearing	les	vêtements	the	clothes
	je voudrais		I would like		vingt		twenty
un	jean		jeans		violet		lilac
	jeudi		Thursday				

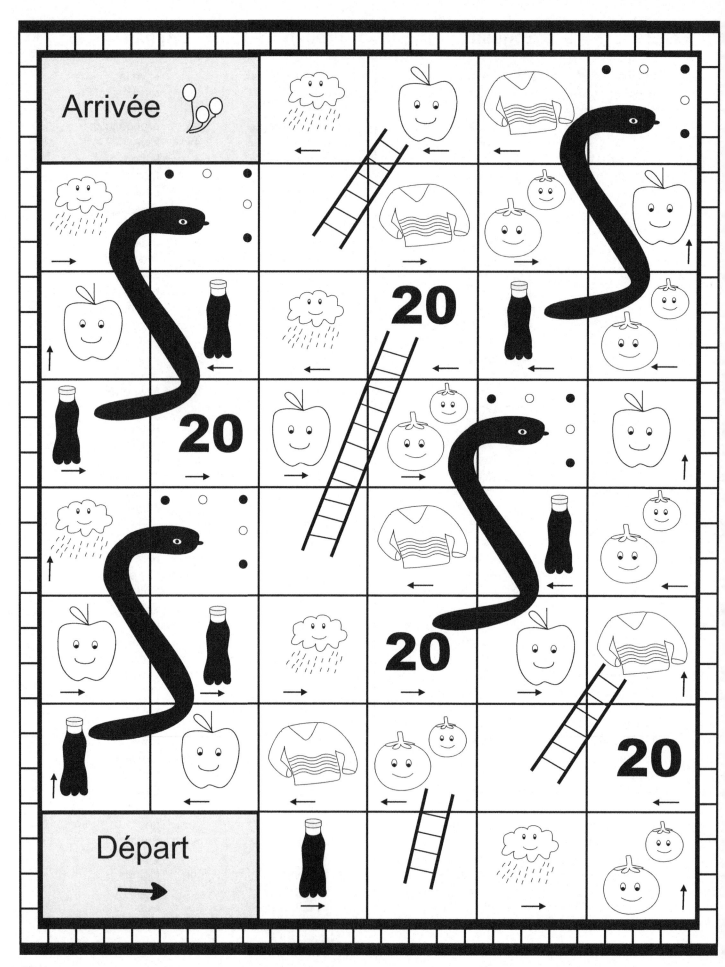

Snakes & ladders game

For this game, you will need a dice and a counter for each player. The counters could be rubbers, cubes or you could make your own on pieces of paper.

How to play

Start at "Départ", roll the dice and count that number of squares.

If the final square has the bottom of the ladder in it go up it, or if it has the head of a snake go down it.

Say the word for the picture you land on in French.

Take turns to roll the dice. To win, arrive first at "Arrivée".

un coca
(a coke)

un pull
(a jumper)

vingt
(twenty)

une pomme
(an apple)

il pleut
(it's raining)

des tomates
(some tomatoes)

Games are a fun way to learn a foreign language! If you like games you could try the book: French Word Games - Cool Kids Speak French

Answers

Page 2

1) un thé   2) une limonade   3) une eau minérale   4) un coca
5) un coca light   6) un jus d'orange   7) un café

Page 3

The following drinks should be drawn in the speech bubbles:
1) a coke   2) a lemonade   3) a coffee   4) a mineral water   5) a tea   6) an orange juice

Page 4

1) Je voudrais un coca, s'il vous plaît.   5) Je voudrais un coca light, s'il vous plaiît.
2) Je voudrais une limonade, s'il vous plaît.   6) Je voudrais un thé, s'I vous plaît.
3) Je voudrais un café, s'il vous plaît.   7) Je voudrais une eau minérale, s'il vous plaît.
4) Je voudrais un Orangina, s'il vous plaît.

Page 5

six limonades   trois thés
sept cocas   quatre cafés
cinq jus d'orange   huit eaux

Page 6

```
        É F A C

J           U     É
U           A   H
S     E   T
D
, C O C A C O L A
O
R           L I G H T
A
N L I M O N A D E
G
E   B O I S S O N
  A N I G N A R O
```

Page 9

Masculine words:	Feminine words:
un melon	une banane
un kiwi	une orange
un citron	une pomme
	une poire
	une fraise

Page 10

The fruit should be coloured as follows:

a red apple   a yellow banana
a brown kiwi   a red strawberry
a yellow lemon   a green melon
a green apple   a green pear

Page 11

The following should be drawn:

3 apples   5 oranges   2 bananas
8 strawberries   9 kiwis
4 lemons   6 pears   7 melons

Page 12

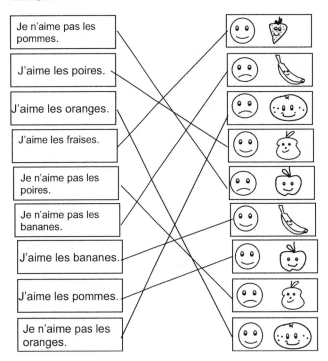

Page 13

	Fruit they like	Fruit they don't like
Sophie	apples & pears	strawberries
Marc	bananas & oranges	pears
Anne	strawberries & kiwis	bananas

Page 14

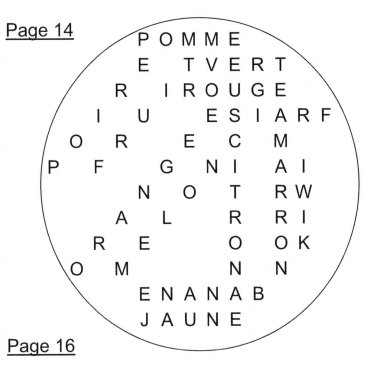

Page 16

a) onze   b) seize   c) vingt   d) dix-sept   e) quinze   f) dix-huit   g) douze

Page 17

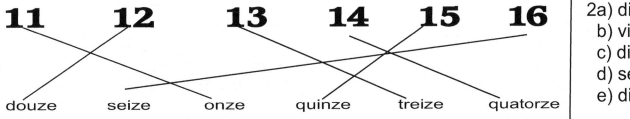

2a) dix-huit
  b) vingt
  c) dix-sept
  d) seize
  e) dix-neuf

Page 18

The balloon should be coloured as follows:

Balloon number 20 in light blue
Balloon number 16 in light brown
Balloon number 11 in dark brown

Balloon number 12 in dark green
Balloon number 18 in dark blue
Balloon number 13 in light grey

Page 19

20	vingt
19	dix-neuf
18	dix-huit
17	dix-sept
16	seize
15	quinze
14	quatorze
13	treize
12	douze
11	onze
10	dix
9	neuf
8	huit
7	sept
6	six
5	cinq
4	quatre
3	trois
2	deux
1	un

Page 20

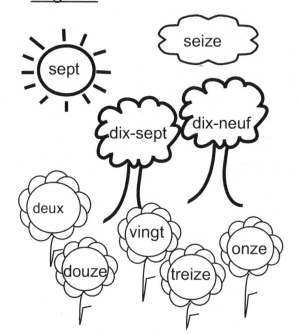

Page 21

Page 24

Page 25

1) Sophie
2) Marc
3) Sophie
4) Anne
5) Marc
6) Anne
7) Marc & Anne

Page 26

Lundi il fait beau.
Mardi il fait chaud.
Mercredi il y a du soleil.
Jeudi il pleut.
Vendredi il neige.
Samedi il fait mauvais.
Dimanche il fait froid.

Page 27

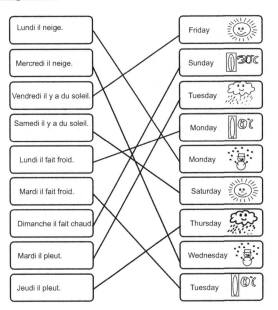

Lundi il neige.	Friday ☀
Mercredi il neige.	Sunday 30°C
Vendredi il y a du soleil.	Tuesday ☁🌧
Samedi il y a du soleil.	Monday 0°C
Lundi il fait froid.	Monday ⛄
Mardi il fait froid.	Saturday ☀
Dimanche il fait chaud.	Thursday ☁🌧
Mardi il pleut.	Wednesday ⛄
Jeudi il pleut.	Tuesday 0°C

Page 28

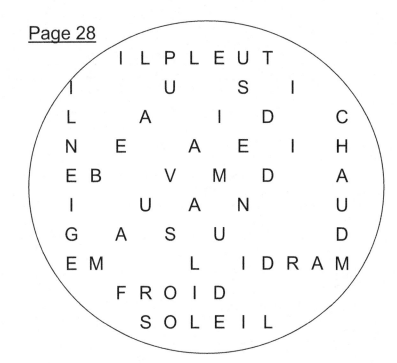

```
        I L P L E U T
    I           U       S       I
    L       A       I   D       C
    N   E       A       E   I   H
    E B     V       M   D       A
    I       U       A   N       U
    G   A       S   U           D
    E M         L       I D R A M
        F R O I D
        S O L E I L
```

Page 30

1) un short   2) un pull   3) une jupe   4) un pantalon   5) un manteau
6) un jean   7) un t-shirt   8) une robe   9) une casquette

Page 31

The pictures should be coloured as follows:
a yellow t-shirt   blue jeans
green shorts   a brown jumper
grey trousers   a pink t-shirt
a red t-shirt   a black coat

Page 32

The pictures should be coloured as follows:
a yellow cap   a grey cap
a green cap   a blue cap
a red dress   a lilac dress
a black and white skirt   a pink skirt

Page 33

a) Je porte un pantalon et un pull.
b) Je porte un t-shirt et une jupe.
c) Je porte un pull et un jean.
d) Je porte un manteau.
e) Je porte un t-shirt et un short.
f) Je porte une robe.

Page 34

```
    P A N T A L O N
S       E T T E U Q S A C
H   V Ê T E M E N T S
O       N                   V
R   A       B L A N C       E
T E         J A U N E       R
J N   M A N T E A U T       L
  O               E   E L   B
  I     E       B   G U     L
  R P           O   U P     E
  U         R   O           U
J               R T R I H S T
```

Page 37

	(face)	(mushroom)	(cheese)	(square)	(round)
Thomas			✓	✓	
Marie	✓		✓		
Luc		✓		✓	
Anne	✓				✓
Paul		✓	✓	✓	✓

Page 38

1a) du citron
b) du sucre
c) des fraises
d) de la crème
e) du chocolat

2a) sucre
b) chocolat
c) citron
d) fraises

Page 39

a) Je voudrais une crêpe avec du chocolat, s'il vous plaît.
b) Je voudrais une crêpe avec des fraises, s'il vous plaît.
c) Je voudrais une crêpe avec du sucre, s'il vous plaît.
d) Je voudrais une crêpe avec de la crème, s'il vous plaît.
e) Je voudrais une crêpe avec du citron, s'il vous plaît.

Page 40

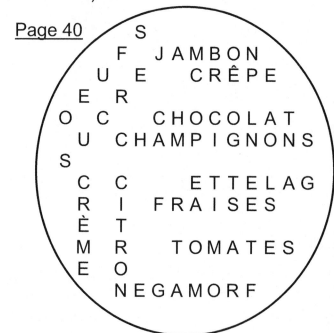

I hope you have enjoyed the fun activities in this book! Try to look back at the French words from time to time to help you remember them.

Reviews help other readers discover my books so please consider leaving a short review on the site where the book was purchased. Your feedback is important to me. Thank you! And have fun learning French! It's a lovely language to learn!

Joanne Leyland

For more information about learning French and the great books by Joanne Leyland go to **https://funfrenchforkids.com**

For information about learning French, Spanish, German, Italian or English as a foreign language go to **https://learnforeignwords.com**

For children learning French there are also the following books by Joanne Leyland:

Photocopiable Games For Teaching French

Differentiated activities for children of various abilities. The games are colour coded according to the amount of French words in each game.

Games include:
- board games
- Dominoes
- snakes and ladders
- 3 or 4 in a row
- co-ordinates
- mini cards

Topics include:
- Pets
- Colours
- Numbers
- Fruit
- Drinks
- Food
- Clothes
- Sport

On Holiday In France Cool Kids Speak French

Ideal for holidays and to challenge children to speak French whilst away. Topics include greetings, numbers, drinks, food, souvenirs, town, hotels & campsites.

French Word Games

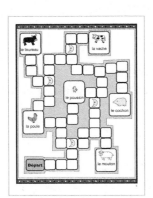

Have fun learning French with this lovely collection of games. The 15 topics include the body, the farm, fruit, the park, the picnic, town, weather, transport…

40 French Word Searches Cool Kids Speak French

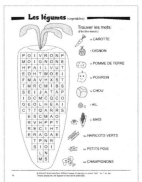

The word searches appear in fun shapes and pictures accompany the French words so that each word search can be a meaningful learning activity. 40 Topics.

Cool Kids Do Maths In French

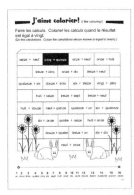

A fantastic way for children to learn 1 to 100 in French.

Great cross curricular resource.

May be photocopied.

Topics include
- Numbers 1 - 10
- Numbers 11 - 20
- Numbers 21 - 40
- Numbers 41 - 60
- Numbers 60 - 80
- Numbers 80 -100
- Fractions

For more information about learning French and the great books by Joanne Leyland go to **https://funfrenchforkids.com**

French

Young Cool Kids Learn French
French Colouring Book For Kids Ages 5 - 7
First Words In French Teacher's Resource Book
Stories for 3-7 year olds: Jack And The French Languasaurus - Books 1, 2 & 3,
Daniel And The French Robot - Books 1, 2 & 3, Sophie And The French Magician
Cool Kids Speak French - Books 1, 2 & 3 *(for kids ages 7 - 11)*
French Word Games - Cool Kids Speak French
Photocopiable Games For Teaching French
40 French Word Searches Cool Kids Speak French
First 100 Words In French Coloring Book Cool Kids Speak French
French at Christmas time
On Holiday In France Cool Kids Speak French
Cool Kids Do Maths In French
Stories in French: Un Alien Sur La Terre, Le Singe Qui Change De Couleur, Tu As Un Animal?

Italian

Young Cool Kids Learn Italian
Italian Colouring Book For Kids Ages 5 - 7
Cool Kids Speak Italian - Books 1, 2 & 3 *(for kids ages 7 - 11)*
Italian Word Games - Cool Kids Speak Italian
Photocopiable Games For Teaching Italian
40 Italian Word Searches Cool Kids Speak Italian
First 100 Words In Italian Coloring Book Cool Kids Speak Italian
On Holiday In Italy Cool Kids Speak Italian
Stories in Italian: Un Alieno Sulla Terra, La Scimmia Che Cambia Colore, Hai Un Animale Domestico?

German

Young Cool Kids Learn German
German Colouring Book For Kids Ages 5 - 7
Sophie And The German Magician *(a story for 3-7 year olds)*
Cool Kids Speak German - Books 1, 2 & 3 *(for kids ages 7 - 11)*
German Word Games - Cool Kids Speak German
Photocopiable Games For Teaching German
40 German Word Searches Cool Kids Speak German
First 100 Words In German Coloring Book Cool Kids Speak German

Spanish

Young Cool Kids Learn Spanish
Spanish Colouring Book For Kids Ages 5 - 7
First Words In Spanish Teacher's Resource Book
Stories for 3-7 year olds: Jack And The Spanish Dinosaur, Sophie And The Spanish Magician,
Daniel And The Spanish Robot - Books 1, 2 & 3
Cool Kids Speak Spanish - Books 1, 2 & 3 *(for kids ages 7 - 11)*
Spanish Word Games - Cool Kids Speak Spanish
Photocopiable Games For Teaching Spanish
40 Spanish Word Searches Cool Kids Speak Spanish
First 100 Words In Spanish Coloring Book Cool Kids Speak Spanish
Spanish at Christmas time
On Holiday In Spain Cool Kids Speak Spanish
Cool Kids Do Maths In Spanish
Stories in Spanish: Un Extraterrestre En La Tierra, El Mono Que Cambia De Color, Seis Mascotas

English as a second language / foreign language

English For Kids Ages 5 - 7
English Colouring Book For Kids Ages 5 - 7
Cool Kids Speak English - Books 1, 2 & 3 *(for kids ages 7 - 11)*
First Words In English - 100 Words To Colour & Learn
English Word Games
Fun Word Search Puzzles